CHANGING THE CHANNEL

BY: HURSHEL VICTOR RICKS II

MR HURSHEL VICTOR RICKS II

Dedicated to Natasha Nyla Cause

January 25, 1997 - October 3, 2021

Changing The Channel was written while in a long term substance abuse program at FMRS, The Oaks, in Beckley, West Virginia between November 17, 2022 and February 17, 2023. Changing The Channel is filled with poems, raps, affirmations, journals, and more.

Also, it is important to know that battling and living with addiction is not linear but zigzag. With this being said, the writings in Changing The Channel are not in

MR HURSHEL VICTOR RICKS II

order from beginning to end.

I HOPE, WISH AND PRAY THAT THIS BOOK HELPS YOU TO CHANGE THE CHANNEL OF YOUR LIFE TO GET YOU...

1. Addiction doesn't care if you've been to the Super Bowl or have soup in your bowl. It doesn't hear a quarter drop on the turnpike toll or who snitched and told. Never has addiction asked for a no or a yes or feel at fault in a field with a track or tracks filling your soul. Addiction walks on the hot sands and sits on mountain coals, doesn't sleep under the moon or wait for the bloom of a rose. Please don't subtract my worth for my substance abuse addiction. I owe myself for each step I took to enter the rehabilitation admissions. I completed the intake, this is not a game or

show, no edited out takes, just me as who I am, for the better, I've survived my worst, I just had a One on One with myself for Christ sake.

2. Today's my Dad's birthday and my blood work is being given. From CBC to HIV, as of now my results are hidden. The phlebotomist used my right arm, but the left side of my body is in pain, stages of sharp pains followed by numbness. O'm not sure if my mind is playing tricks on me or if my body is dealing with a 25-year-old drug use sentence. On top of that, I ate cheese, it was pepperoni pizza, now my lactose intolerance is in its feelings. It's not even 6 o'clock. No smokes for the next smoke thirty. Well, if I can't fight off the cocaine and alcohol, then the cigs withdrawal shouldn't be too dirty. Last night was my first A.A. class group and I hope I make it to the the second. As for now, I'll take it one day at time. I'm on step one and I need not to rush the next eleven. And, I still don't know if living with nerve damage in my mouth is a curse or a blessing. For now, I'm resting in my bed in The Oaks. I guess that means Da Front Porch is nesting.

3. Today the interviewer, tomorrow photographer. Next day, cameraman, this ain't no abra-ca-dabra. Hustle smart with

dedication and wake up on time. Go to sleep in the morning and be up by nine. Two more charges in the bag, can't leave nothing to chance. Don't wanna have a million dollar blink with a dead Sony flash. I gotta interview rappers, like Da Front Porch don't rap. They said be careful in the hood, like Da Front Porch never trapped.

4. What's up, how you doin', I'm new around town
I know we met a couple weeks back, I'm
worried bout 3 months from now
You see me, I'm really leaning on staying longer than a hour
I'm a give 100% at The Oaks, you know 101 South Eisenhower
And if I slip and fall please don't just sit there and let me fail
I'll be your crutch in need, just like you, I gotta story to tell.

5. Don't pass me a bottle unless it's water
Yeah, I mean water, H20, water
Doc said my liver good
Don't know how when I'm a life time partier
And felony-free, let me pop my own collar.

6. I'm a master like Splinter,
I'm not a rat, there's a difference
Serious face like I'm constipated
Telling you only what it is, like I'm Yoda.

7. Do you remember the time when we took that walk?
It was to you show you your future.
Do you remember the time we went to G-5 before dark?
It was to share my dreams with you.
Did you know everything you create to me is a precious moment?
That's why I sacrificed my right arm.
You're the mermaid I always cherished from the
Island Drive to the tropical storm.
I study all that you do.
Why else would I be at University.
And every September is another year of your existence.
The shores of Jamaica is your birthplace.
I keep a map on my side like air to a lung.
Even left an iPhone turned on with GPS on
Just in case you came aboard.
I've seen you 3 times face to face
Although No One believes me.
Why, when you're sweeter than a ripe mango.
A rare delicacy.
What I would do to share my life with you.
My love for you is never ending.
I'll keep searching for who I cherish
Like a jelly fish streaming.
Only God knows the beauties you possess,
And God told me so.

So I've packed all my bags
And I'm ready to go.
Back to the white beach sands of Miami
Where you've last been seen
And I pray that when I find you,
I'll be all that you dreamed.

She's a cute hottie with everything right
If I see her again, she'll be Hursh's for life
I've traveled the oceans, seas and bays for all of my life.
I want a mermaid to cherish all of my life.

I wanna marry who I cherish.
Enjoy her life like Sprite.
Her skin tone is golden.
Her melanin shines bright.
I lied to her twice in my life.
She cursed me out twice.
And I ain't even mad,
She set Da Front Porch right.
She's so popular.
She's cherished for real.
From Nicki in New York,
To Trina at the crib
Know's who she is.
Bruh, I love her for real.

She's the ornament on the tree.

A once in a lifetime gift for real.

You can't tell me what not to do

Or not how to feel.

I wanna seal the deal

She's a Miami doll for real.

Even the Dolphins know

Cherish for real.

I'm not a cheetah or dance like a penguin,

That's for real.

I like to write my wrongs,

And write my rights.

I rather cook than fight.

See her morning smile orange juice bright

Because she shines all day

And a star all night,

But she'll never know how I feel,

Because I'm shy and won't record on the mic.

She's a cute hottie with everything right

If I see her again, she'll be Hursh's for life

I've traveled the oceans, seas and bays for all of my life.

I want a mermaid to cherish all of my life.

Do you hear what I hear?

Do you see what I see?

Do you know what I know?
Cherished moments at Da Front Porch.

8. Keep it honest before they start playing trumpets.
Don't know one care if it's Thanksgiving.
Play chicken, you get dumplings.
The streets'll eat you up if you act sweet Lil' Debbie.
Everybody wanna be number one, just don't be 24/7 petty.
Ready. Set. Go. First down, touchdown,
Keep ya head above water, take a breath before you stroke.
You don't wanna drown,
Be joke of the year, no class, just clown.
To lose all your respect in just one minute,
Just to be down.
Everybody knows you have flaw. Switch seasons.
Don't fall. Just spring.

9. A million dollar blink starts with a polished out dream.
Remember you owe you. That's what my momma told me.
And she the real O.G.
I had to washout my eyes just to clean out my team.
Or to be laid to rest with trumpets playing would of been mine.
Am I living the American Dream or S-U-R-V-I-V-I-N-G.
Last night was peanut butter and jelly.

It was strawberry. I felt preserved.

And I realized all the spoons were dirty.

Ever had cereal with a fork? It just ain't the same thing.

Now you tell me there's not a thin line between
Surviving and the American Dream.

10. Now say it with me, drug-free is how I choose to be.

Drug-Free, I can see it clearly now.

Drug-Free, the change starts with me.

1,2,3… Today, I'm drug-free.

11. Character is tested when you're up against it.

I want you to hold on a little longer.

Take a deep breath, walk a little stronger.

Be the best version to you.

Remember your name.

Don't just change the game. Create the game.

Make them remember your name.

Don't cash out for fame. Everybody's cashing out.

Keep your eyes on the prize.

Humility is first prize. Make 'em recognize.

Church is where your soul revives. Pay your tithes.

Free your mind and the rest will follow.

Don't forget the time we have is a present,
most importantly borrowed.

12. Integrity is to be honest to you and me.
The price to be a decent human being is always free.
The loss of one's life is a loss to the entire community.
As a whole, we must stand strong as a unity.
These streets are cold at night and hot in the day.
Every thing isn't black or white, there's always a shade of gray.
I never claimed to be perfect, only know how to be me.
It just hurts seeing my people in pain.
Here's a breath of freedom of speech.
In my letter to The Oaks, I just want to say thank you.
God, you saved my life. Now it's my turn to plant a tree.
I owe myself and you owe you.
This is bigger than me. I must be the root.
This is the last time…the world I will use.
And the world is loose, because it's about growth.
So shame the devil and tell the truth.

13. Today with the windchill it is negative 30,
And this is at 4:15 with the sunshine.
I thank God my family sent me a winter coat, gloves and mask.
My coffee chilled instantly.
And this is the first week of winter.
Still I smile. Still I am glad. Still I pray.

Life don't owe you nothing. You owe it to yourself.
Don't get drunk and mad just to end up more drunk and mad.
Living a real life thriller filled with drama.

Master peace Mister Bad.

It's time to follow thru and get help.
Pull your pants up, here's a belt.
Life ain't a steak, it's at stake.
Don't waste your cheese, don't let it melt.
This is real talk, heart felt.
Weigh your options, read your scale.
This ain't bout liking you.
This is about loving you. This is about owing you.
Looking at the man in the mirror saying, "I love you."

14. Packard said the camera is worse than the gun.
You already heard the saying,
A picture is worth a thousand verbs.
But I'm not the one making you see the same thing, the same way, at the same time
Without your moments of time to educate your mind, not manipulate your mind.

Hustle smart when you grind.
Hustle smart, I bet you shine.

Don't let this fool you, I wear glasses to see,
I choose to never walk blind.

Even the most beautiful places are often the most dangerous.

Instead of kill or be killed, why not love to stay alive.

That should be the natural thrill.

And accept the fact it's hard to kill what you can't see because time is your most dangerous enemy.

So don't make the next vacation, the longest vacation of your life.

Don't fall for the banana in the tail pipe.

15. There is nothing wrong with loving yourself.

Don't park your dreams on a shelf.

Speak your wants and needs into existence.

If the race is 3/4 mile, go for a full mile, the extra distance.

If we're going to survive we have to trust each other, grow with each other, co-exist.

You can eat one fish today or learn how to fish.

Be a winner, stay strong. At times, life will seem rough.

Keep your faith in God, for God is Love.

Please forgive me for being away.

Just know my love for you is unconditional.

And I pray for your health, peace and happiness every night as I pray.

It shouldn't of taken this long to clean out my

closet and begin to write my wrongs.

I just want you to know I learned the difference between a house and a home.

16. First down, touch down, go the whole distance.

Never been to N.Y., but I seen the Hell's kitchen.

Everybody wanna be in the major league ain't made for pitchin'.

Get it done A.S.A.P., like it's nobody's business.

Stop waiting for the in-crowd for a witness.

These days you don't rely on twenty year pensions.

You get what you put in. Eat a chicken or be a chicken.

Get up out my bubble space, don't need your likes and mentions.

Had to put myself on timeout, ain't want the penitentiary.

Everyday above ground is a gift, before and after Christmas.

Keep it clean like a Chevy 70's droptop on 20-something inches.

Had to work my mind and body, I'm a true planet fitness.

And the ladies still love me, wanting Hursh kisses.

Da Front Porch Association ain't going out of business.

Da Front Porch lit, livid, limitless and luxuriously livin'.

Mama said it be trials like this

Got on my knees, said a prayer, not a wish.

Had to get a pole, hit the ocean and fish.

First down, touchdown, had to make it make sense.

17. Gotta get things back in order, like right right right now.
Gas the whip, get in motion, you driving, like right right now.
I know she bad, that's why you sweatin' she
wit' me, like right right now.
Twist the game one mo' time, like right right right now.
My dawg in the feds and headed home, like right right right now.
Real shit I fell off, got too high and now I'm
good, like right right now.
Ain't here shit nobody said, they thought I
was dead , like right right now.
Ain't no hoe in me. I'm pushing for greatness, like right right now.
Loss the condo 15 floors high and I don't
need it, like right right now.
I need the Cherish. Need the ink on my side, like right right now.
Need to quit the squares, switch to diamonds,
I'm vibin', like right right now.
You get no pound, you get no love if you
flakin', like right right now.
I'm still watchin' the puddikat, like right right right now.
And I keep my mind on my money, money
over bitches, like right right now.
Should hit the studio booth and record
this hit , like right right now.
Da Front Porch done snap, he back, like right right now.
He don't rap, he don't trap, that's what they
saying, like right right now.

CHANGING THE CHANNEL

Who got ya radio jumpin' and bumpin', like right right now.

Clubs showing love, and I ain't drink, like right right now.

Tight jeans, somethin' fine on me, like right right now.

Sweetie mean and living the dream, like right right now.

I'm seeing that you jealous and envy, like right right now.

Ain't got time for your envy and jealousy, like right right now.

Who got that quarter pounder with extra cheese, like right right now.

I got that quarter pounder, look at me cheese, like right right now.

Had to hustle smart, everybodies cashin' out, like right right now.

They say I'm too old to be hitting' the stag, like right right now.

Ain't to old to keep my pockets fluffy, like right right now.

Hursh went galactic on rockets, like right right now.

Got my money on the Heat and the Dolphins, like right right now.

I'm from the 305 where it's live 24/7, like right right now.

But I be chillin' in the 304 where it's breezy, like right right now.

Lookin' in the mirror, glad to see me, like right right now.

Don't need no beef with you cowards, you see me, like right right now.

Jumpin' on yo' couch, so shut yo' mouth, like right right now.

18. Too many children relapsed, dying. Mothers and Pops cryin'.

News reporting true lies, we believin' the true lies.

Churches demanding tithes, can't get a job with no tie.

In life there's no ties, doing the right thing, and still die.

Nana asked the Lord why her son on drugs now.
Prayin' he find hope, and stop walkin' on disguised mines.
Where juice turns to wine, distorting our own minds.
While they sayin' we'll be fine, time after time.
Where everybody on go mode, pressin' the cheat code.
Chasin' last nights dream, trapped in a snow globe.
Fools not even paraplegic, won't even stand on they own ten toes.
Robbin' to have gold, rappin' our mind in no goals.
Pushin' dope in our brains, walkin' on tracks
towards a speeding train.
Pawnin' our own soul, not knowin' we breakin' our own mold.
In life where there's moles, plotting' on our hope.
In reality, we're our own mole, livin' in a world that's so cold.

As for me, I'm livin' righteous, tomorrow's no guarantee.
It's a 52-card pick up in life's 360 degrees.
I'm thankful for the sunshine and blessed to feel the breeze.
Prayer starts in your soul, self-love is always free.

Now it's time to stand tall, winter, spring, summer and fall.
Don't be scared, make that call, just not to get raw.
At times I was Paul, yes, I admit I have flaws.
But with God on my side, my sight is clear now.
Letting him coach me, call after call, not scared to control the ball.
If life was suppose to be easy, faith wouldn't know us at all.
Removing can't from my words, and no's from my journeys.

CHANGING THE CHANNEL

I might just have a chance to not be on today's gurney.

But if I do die and God calls me home, I'll be thankful
and grateful to enter the pearly gates.

With God, it's never too late to have love and limitless faith.

I'm no actor, don't need a Tony to say life was great.

Even with the pitfalls, pains and life stakes, I still
put up my fence and gave my yard a rake,

To keep my world tidy and clean with no snakes.

And with my last breath, at the last moon, I didn't fall for the bait.

As for me, I'm livin' righteous, tomorrow's no guarantee.

It's a 52-card pick up in life's 360 degrees.

I'm thankful for the sunshine and blessed to feel the breeze.

Prayer starts in your soul, self-love is always free.

I was just getting my life in order, when
life ordered a different deal.

9 P.M., we were kissing, 1 A.M., your life was still.

I know God called you home, but why on our wedding day.

Our wedding shower was in D.C., Tasha and
Hursh, at the Hirschorn Museum.

We have art in the museum, she even had my daughter's
mother to do her hair, ask her if you don't believe me.

Seems like right after she passed, my world
drowned to worse from bad.

I found a a friend in a drink and crack, then
boot, and some nights, the smack.

Yeah I had a crib, it wasn't a home, just stating facts.

Some days I skipped a shower, most nights I skipped a meal.
My family, they tried to help, my heart just wouldn't hear.
My dreams were drowned in tears, and death I did not fear.
Invited pain inside my home, my heart, my voice and ears.
My friends, most of them women, would check on me day to day.
It broke their hearts to see Hursh da Front
Porch in pain in every way.
You said the sun was shining, to me, everyday was gray.
Felt like I was being punished, even forgot how to pray.

As for me, I'm livin' righteous, tomorrow's no guarantee.
It's a 52-card pick up in life's 360 degrees.
I'm thankful for the sunshine and blessed to feel the breeze.
Prayer starts in your soul, self-love is always free.

19. Got me a valley chic, straight up bootlegger.
Size 5, love pink, and everything leopard.
Dopeboys wanna get her, she ain't fallin' for they cheddar.
She know who won the race, she love the third leg.
She know I stay ahead, and she really love my head.
I hustle smart so I get her, her personal Zig Ziglar.
I'm a playa, she a playette, you can stay and take our picture.
The way she play the game, like a phlebotomist.
Every word brings pressure to you off brand pricks.

And she bring the money back home, I know you see the print.
The way she make it pop, is like winter green mint.
Her walks a jagged edge, it must be Heaven
sent, it took time to build this.
Something mystic like the Nile and Egyptian pyramid.
She stay up on the mountain, Puerto Rican-ish.
Talkin' bout my real live, love savage secret.

I'm no slim lip shitz, I carry my own weight.
3,2,1 spin the wheel, we make days out of dates.
I put the ice on her cakes, taking pictures, hide the face.
Sour apple tastes good, Miss Shhh tastes great.
Still nobody knows our plays, grand slam the whole pink.
Hit first, hit second, hit third, home plate.
No errors, always fresh, no fish, no stinks.
Super clean, stays tight, drips wet, stays shaved.
I'm known to be a pirate on her Caribbean wave.
And when we step out, we make the Earth quake.
She has the son of God, why are you so amazed.
That a guy named Hursh Vick gotta pretty smile babe.
I mean she gotta pretty smile, you know what I'm tryin' to say.
It was a pleasure to open her safe, it was well worth the wait.
How she showed me that treasure made me great on my feet.
Bet big, bet better, I'm a winner not a failure.

I love you in a way that I have never loved before.

You never left me when I was down and out,
you love me for rich and poor.

I want to build a life with you, who knows, we can open a store.

Add a few slot machines, and you already know what for.

You ain't never called me Hursh, to you, I've always been Vick.

I miss riding' shotgun with you on our Bonnie and Clyde trips.

You don't eat meat, and you know I love shrimp. Let's
hit the dance floor, so I can say, dip baby dip.

Wherever we go, we go hard 100 percent, or nothing at all.

You're Five-one and a half, and make me feel tall.

When I shop, we shop, from Walmart to the mall.

You're more than a stallion, you deserve the galaxy, not a stall.

When I hit you on the iPhone for a FaceTime to wake you.

You say let me brush my teeth, and I'll be there in 20 to get you.

I remember when we met New Year's Eve at the club.

Went from a night at Lust to making love in this club.

20. As painful as it sounds if I had to change a
thing, I wouldn't change a thing.

Because it wouldn't of made me the man that I am.

From every clean hundred to every dirty grind,
this was all part of God's plan.

Who am I to stop the hour glass sand, to give my life's story a ban.

This doesn't mean I don't live in a world of
should of could of, would of's.

Like I should of never gottin' in the ride that night.

CHANGING THE CHANNEL

Or I could of stood tall and I fight.

Or I would of gottin' on my knees and cried.

The wisdom I gained from living my life.

Searching for a shining light on Earth's dark night.

I'm man enough to admit my wrongs.

Sometimes I went left, just to be right.

Other times I went left, when I should of went right.

The knowledge of power to teach others what I learned throughout life is the epitome of a missionary at best if I'm right.

I had to open my ears, mind and heart, just for a 20/20 sight.

21. Pick locks, feel the Ziploc, fill the Ziploc fatter than a zit on the tip of your chin, pop.

This here a wrist watch, diamonds dance non-stop.

45 on my side, I bust yo ass, that's hip hop.

Yo can't take your bitch back, I'll rent her for the right price.

She may of used to love your ass, shit, not tonight.

So watch your mouth, you already lost the bitch, don't lose your life.

You gotta a case of bitch-idis, more common than arthritis.

Now you sad in the face, thinking you might as well gone and kill ya self, and me too, shit, I'm not the virus.

I'm more like the pilot, known to lift her up.

Keep her steady, and lay her down, who the flyest.

That's why she ridin', do or dyin', right beside me.

Stay in line, I ain't lying, I ain't sorry.

I got game, if you had game, it would be the game of sorry.

Now move, you're out of time, I'm on borrowed time.

And I ain't tryin' to do no time for you haters.

Grow a back bone, get a spine, and you'll do just fine.

One more thing fool, just know what you playin', who you playin', why you playin'.

The bottom line is this, as for me, I will always go all in for Love and Happiness.

22. Courage means heart in latin. Have the courage to be imperfect. Being vulnerable makes you beautiful. A little breakdown can feel like a big breakdown if you focus on the negative. Life is neither good or bad. It just is what it is. Fighting against vulnerability is a battle you won't win. Have the courage to love yourself with out hurting others. Make the uncertain, certain. Don't be afraid to have a conversation. Don't be afraid to learn. Don't pretend what you do does not affect others. Be authentic. Say sorry and fix it. Love with your whole heart with no guarantee in return. Have a conversation with others and yourself at the same time. Vulnerability is not a weakness. Being vulnerable opens up a space for a person to have an opinion about you which takes a lot of courage to listen to others opinion and not to be close-minded and to not stop an opportunity to grow. As Brene' Brown said, "Vulnerability is the birthplace of innovations, creativity and change."

23. Don't over think, it's about progress. Negative thinking breeds negative thinking emotions even when there are gains which can make people not give their selves credit for positive changes or even recognize positive changes with out reminding theirselves

of all the negative changes instead of motivating theirselves from the positive changes of life.

24. I'll never forget the good times.
It's hard write what's on my mind.
I guess the wind that blows are your words.
That's what's on my mind.
Your smile is the sunshine.
Together, they bring peace.
I was your backbone.
You massaged my spine.
At the drop of a dime.
I watched you grow into a woman.
So kind, so divine.

25. You keep telling me that I got everything.
I got everything, except you.

26. I am stronger than what I was.

27. With recovery, there is a responsibility of service. The service is to sure my experiences in meetings as well as help build AA/NA groups by something as small as making

coffee for the meetings. By making myself as important part of the AA/ NA group, it allows me to be available to connect with new or current members. Also, while I am trying to help others, there may be issues I am dealing with that other members may be able to help me out with.

28. Fuck wit' me you be dead by 1, stop playin' with me.
Ain't gotta move from my desk, make one call, you're gone easily.
Big dawgs on deck for you pussies, cat-tas-tro-phe.
Going bonkers in the trenches, you loose the war, now pay me.
We shoot, change, cover, shoot change,
cover. The military mind in me.
Welcome to no mans land, feeding you pain and misery.
I talk, you listen, if the sunrise you wanna see.
Fool, when the sun set, bodies get wet,
funeral homes thankin' me.
Leavin' faces charred, mouths wired, and whole lives scarred.
Bullets flying like birds, burning bodies hot like tar.
See you made it this far, you must of lift weights, heavy bars.
You wanna keep going, raise up, stand high to be a star.
This ain't golf, there's no pars, just play your part.
We hit hard, bomb cars, real life movie stars.
My life scarred, tatted hearts, a dreamed czar.
To be a connoisseur, revolutionary man of
power, just to be number one.
Had to lay low in The Oaks, just to rebuild, set for another kill.

With a clear conscious, ain't dealing with non-sense, my word is the shield.
There's so much snow in the field, you'll go numb from the feel.
Each stroke is a kill at will, I got 52 more reasons to make a deal.
90 days later, the war ain't over, here, sit, check the mil.
No spoons, all knives, shit at stake, get you a meal.
More room for May, Memorial chills.
Ain't no replays. You get boxed laying in the shade of shields.
I make no promises in my life, just guarantees for the day.
Stay clean, stay paid and away from the afraid.
Every 24 hours the game plan starts the same.
Ain't rockin' with ya. I'm reppin' till my heart shines of Jade.
Ain't dealing with ya strange, beating up your campaign.
Keeping it 100 percent at all times, O.J. not no Tang.
And the round goes chitty-chitty, bang bang, chitty-chitty, bang bang.
Keep your head up or get lost tossing change just be number one.

29. To be alive is greatness, for self-love has no wait-list.
Find faith, keep faith, share faith, humility brings patience.
Being humble is a 24-hour paid shift, you have to work at it.
It's like growing static, yielding thru traffic, all while in wrinkle-free fabric.

30. Make the changes in your life that you need as if your life depended on it. Have someone supporting you that believes in you

as much or more than you believe in your self. Some things that you have to do on your own still needs the help of others.

31. So many nights I cried tears of confusion.
Cocaine-induced visions making my real life polluted.
Losing who left invited dates with meth.
Went from counting my blessings, to adding unwarranted stress.
I wasn't tip-toeing with death, I was racing to the grave.
Fast-paced, double-pace, a slow suicide is what I chased.
From a garden of dreams, to weeds in my safe.
Breathing smoke from the Drago into my boney structured face.
If this brings you agony and nightmares to your home plate, please keep running, don't slide for the devils's cake.
Open your third eye, reveal your strength today.
Tomorrows no guarantee, go survive to see the next day.
Now I'm 50 pounds wiser, if wisdom has a weight.
And with my eyes closed, I finally became a wake.
No more trembles, no more visuals of my
life in a broke mirror, okay.
I cut the thread from my shoulders...I ain't nobody's bait.

32. I hope that you hear me.
Do you hear me?
I know you're there.

You have to be there.

I need to calm down.

Yeah, you hear me.

You're the one telling me to calm down.

I was gonna ask if you see this smile on my face.

I know you already do.

I mean of course you do, you said you'd always be here with me.

You told me not to be bitter.

What I'm trying to say is that, "I love you."

33. So todays, Just for Today, is about the ideas of fun changing an exchanging events likes nights at local clubs for watching aquatic life like dolphins, days having picnics or attending comedy shows at N.A. meetings. I like this idea. Many comedy shows require 2 minimum drinks and my past picnics involved some type of liquor infused Icee or daiquiri. Also, working and living the nightlife in clubs, I had so much alcohol and drugs because it was available and stated in my contracts to have so much alcohol ready for me and my guests. The drugs were just a perk of the job in some situations. That's one of the wore benefits and gifts of the nightlife. As the words of one of my brothers in sobriety would say, "it was all fun, until it wasn't." I can continue to make music, creatively write, deejay, host events, take photos, film and produce events as well as have picnics , attend comedy shows and enjoy the ocean without drugs or alcohol with the proper precautions. The main reason I will not use substances is because I don't want use drugs or alcohol anymore and I am on a mission with realistic

goals.

34. I can't force you to accept where your life is heading.

Or make you be how you should breathe.

But I will tell you this.

Life will not get any better until you take a sip of honest tea.

Life has two guarantees.

One is that you're born and second is that you die.

What you do in between is how you spend and value your time.

And some days need dusting, just to have a shine.

So use the tool between your two shoulders, I'm talking about your brain, to active your spine.

It is not how you start, it is how you end.

Consider your legacy, day out and day in.

You have to build a foundation, don't forget about the blueprint.

And please drink more honest tea.

Your reputation is based on your acts and the words from your lips.

You know what you've done, where you been, and how you acted.

Please note, there is nothing wrong with making changes.

New environments bring new attractions.

Go get active and be your best advertisement.

35. Don't wear yourself out trying to get rich.

Be wise enough to know when to quit.

To stand up, back in the days, we use to sit.

Sit on the truth, sit on the change, we ain't
need glue to make it stick.

I'm a pro with these verbs, spitting you proverbs.

I'm not feasting with gluttons or carousing with drunkards.

I'm dodging the cardinal sins forever shooting them the birds.

I'm a check what you saw, what you said, and what you heard.

Wisdom is sweet to the soul, hope you find it for a bright future.

You can't switch gears and go forward always sitting in neutral.

Your eyes wondering round the room
wondering who'll do what to ya.

That's what happens when you order up karma,
thinking I won't serve it to ya.

You're an undisciplined child disgracing your own mother.

Spoiled to the bone, ready to be eaten by vultures.

Pause with all ya would of, could of, should of's.

And do a lil' something more just to benefit the culture.

36. It's not about the cigarette.

It's about the fresh air.

It's not about the lighter.

It's about the trees, I love that stare.

It's not about the cheese, I love the turkey or ham.

It's not about being away from home, because
home is where the heart glows.

If I walk outside on my own, it's not because I'm a quitter.

I don't want to be a nuisance, seem to be unthankful or bitter.

I'm just trying to understand why am I being punished.

When all I've done is cared, shared, and for the
first time in a long time, kept it 100.

37. One thing about my past behavior that I am very ashamed of stealing because stealing leads to lying and breaking trust. One fear I have that nobody else is aware of is something I'm not ready to share at this time. One thing that makes me very sad is not being able to make music, take pictures and videos and use a computer while in rehab. One person whom I love dearly is mother. The reason is I love this person is because she loves me unconditionally and she loved me before I loved myself.

38. If I die tonight, let the people know I lived as a man.

I learned to be patient and understanding,
over stepping a grand stand.

Showing my daughter the meaning of a parent,
to be an original and no ones parrot.

Teaching my nephew and niece to eat their
vegetables, and shine like 24 karats.

And if I never get into another relationship, still
live my life as suitor, ready for marriage.

Not ashamed to cook and clean, and protect

the youth with my carriage.

Caring for others, being an obedient usher,
and above all, being a child of God.

And respecting my mother are just a few aspects of being a man.

Let's not forget…creating, starting and completing a plan.

Let's not forget…being humble, and
apologizing when wrong or rude.

Agreeing to disagree, and knowing how to exit a room.

In other words, changing the climate, just
to keep everything cool.

By acting my age and calling a spade a spade.

Knowing why to wear a tie, knowing why I fight who I fade.

Paying my dues by paying my bills, building my family foundation brick by brick, and never breaking the seal.

I was a man when I woke up and prayed.

Tell 'em I said that before my last meal.

39. I am guilty of isolating myself after Tasha passed away. I am ashamed that I isolated myself from myself, my family, and society. What I mean is that I stopped doing things I loved to do that made me who I am. I shut down my id, ego and super-ego many days and nights in many uncomfortable, embarrassing, sad and un-nurturing ways. I didn't have to physically be alone to isolate myself. I isolated myself from my family and friends even when they were around because I was never fully me due

to an unhealthy blend of isolation, shame, guilt, and depression. I had invited people to my life with bad intentions to my life and to people who cared about my life. Since starting my recovery by detoxing at Berkeley Medical Center in Martinsburg, West Virginia (WV) and my current 70-plus days at The Oaks in Beckley, West Virginia I have begun to live again by putting one shoe on at a time and taking one step at a time. I have opened up with other clients, staff, attended outings such as shopping, going to the park and even going to a bowling alley for an activity as well as other arts and crafts. I am even eating three daily meals and my hygiene has drastically improved. I remember attending trips, participating in arts and crafts and doing a lot of shopping leading up to Tasha's death which led to my immediate increase in drug use. I had isolated myself from family. I wouldn't answer phone calls and at times I would would stay the night at the estate and I would still be distant because using drugs and alcohol was at the forefront of my mind. The same restrictions applied to my business. I was in such a dark, unhealthy mental and physical state that I allowed my business to shut down for 16 months. With recovery, things that are important to my id, ego, and super-ego that connect me to society, family and myself have started happening after being obsessed with my sobriety, which has connected me back to my world, I chose to be selfish when it comes to my sobriety and selfless when it comes to my society and family by being a positive, influential person.

40. As for me and my recovery, I am open to the ideas of spiritual connections, therapy, A.A., N.A., self-growth or other programs to build humility, self-sufficiency, self-importance, and self-centeredness to guide me the strength during my recovery.

41. I'm not a doctor but I know that the disease or illness or disorder never applies to me and if all three doctors, therapists, medical professionals, acquaintances, family, friends, and co-workers say otherwise then they are all wrong and I am right. I'm no therapist, and I don't go to therapy and will never go to therapy because therapy is for losers, people who are scared face their issues and people who can't fix their life is in shambles and I have no plan and will not even take advantage of the opportunities to help myself become self- sufficient. What I just told you were the epitome of self-centeredness. Not only did I give examples of turning down opportunities to receive handouts, hand-ups, assistance, advice and support, I also gave examples of how self-centeredness can cause another person to doubt that

their addiction is a disease and to not even acknowledge that a problem exists. I would hope that I, that you, that we would not bankrupt our on self-righteousness but if that is the choice, that I, you or we do not feel so high almighty and absorbed with self-importance that we bring others down.

42. It is unrealistic to expect my family to accept or believe that I am changing just because I said I am. I cannot be upset or angry or have grievances about the rules and regulations my family place on me because of my past actions. For example, having to wait in my truck in front of the house for someone to get home so I can go in the house or my family making random stops at my house and assuming everyone at my home is an addict or a bad influence. I have to accept that my family has the right and proof to question my changes in life, in example, with my addiction to cocaine. Thankfully, my family is supporting me at The Oaks. My family has always wanted me to be great, successful and healthy among other things. My family has noticed some changes in me since I started my recovery and they know I am not doing this just to get by to to manipulate someone. They also considered that I voluntarily chose to make a change and I'm not getting any type of outside reward or removal of punishment for being at The Oaks.

My family know that I am taking my recovery and what I have learned at The Oaks with me because each time I converse with my family, I am going over my exit strategy from The Oaks, as well as telling them about the steps I have taken on my own accord. They see that I am practicing these principles in all of my affairs. Effort goes along way when transitioning from being an embarrassment of a burden to becoming a credit in the family foundation and structure. And while I can't be guaranteed that changes will be noticed, I must still take my recovery everywhere I go.

43. I know more about how to live than I did yesterday but not as much as I'll know tomorrow. Today, I'll learn something. This reminds me of one of the positive thoughts and affirmations that I wrote for myself yesterday. I am not scared to lose today because it gives me something to practice for. One of the next things abut recovery is knowing that we have the power and are gaining the knowledge to rewire ourselves. Changing our mindset as an addict is a survival skill. Learning about human responsibilities and learning how to apply human responsibilities may be able to help us with the isolation and anxiety issues that we may have had as early as childhood or as recent as a problem we may have just had a few moments ago. I think one of the most important things that

we should strive for as a an addict or simply a decent human being is self-growth, and not being content with being okay with where we are to start to believe that we cannot get better, or we have to wait for someone to help us before we start to help ourselves.

44. I will find joy in witnessing the recovery of another. I have seen a person I love with all my heart recover from the use of drugs. At one time, the use of drugs were for fun and then substance abuse was wrapped around depression. Using drugs to try to forget the death of her mother and sister and best friend, between her ages of 19 and 23, the voice of public opinion of a murder she had nothing to do with because a newspaper editor placed her picture front page next to a murder suspect Her spirit was torn even though she had two young daughters. July of 2021, she was with both her young daughter and cleaned herself off drugs and depression and was ready to live again. Her mind, body, and spirit was healthy. In September 2021, we were together all month and we had decided to tie the knot. We both knew about her health situations and she knew I wanted to marry her so that last week of September we went to Washington D.C. for a wedding shower. She did not do any drugs. We had a great time without drugs. On October 2nd we returned to Martinsburg, West Virginia

and on the morning of October 3rd, our wedding date, she passed away. Today, January 25th, 2023 is Tasha's birthday, and she would have turned 26-years-old. I know she is in Heaven being a cheerleader about my sobriety. I see her smile and I feel her hug and I remember why she told me she stopped using and knowing that she shared that information with me is fuel to continue my sobriety even when no one is looking. Talk about an added gift of recovery and a spiritual awakening.

45. Trying to do the next right thing for the right reason has been easier since I have began changing my mindset. I've always cared about others but recently I have began caring for people in a safe way. I'm not risking my safety to help others. I'm doing my best to lead by example and helping people in safe places using morals and values.

46. It feels free to be able to think clearly. I am actually proud of where I am in life and I know that with God and my family, I have the strength and courage to use my talents and gifts to build a foundation for my family to ensure a safe, secure legacy.

47. I was watching Robin Hood starring Jamie Foxx and Jamie

Foxx as John said to Robin Hood, "You're only powerless, if you believe you're powerless." And then, this mornings Just For Today message is: *I admit that I am powerless over my addiction. I will surrender to win.* With my addiction and in life, I must admit defeat to be able to find strength and grow. I'm sure some people will look at what I wrote and say Robin Hood is a fictional story, but someone had to write the dialogue with a purpose, so why should I not rewrite my story and add a chapter called, "After the Defeat." Yesterday, I also watched Grid-Iron BGang, based on a true story, featuring Dwayne "The Rock" Johnson. He played football in real life at "The U" which is the University of Miami Hurricanes. In the movie, one of The Rock's lines was to the football team stating how they lost because this was their first game and that the other team is not 38 points better than them. With my addiction, I admitted that crack-cocaine kicked my ass but crack-cocaine is not better than me. I'm not scared to ask for help with my treatment or issues. I'm a man first and if I could have fixed my problem by myself I would not have been admitted to The Oaks and still be here eight weeks later. I'd be a fool to leave here after completing the program and not give a full effort by being vulnerable and accepting help in new ways and forms from new people and programs without being stubborn, arrogant and causing disruption to the concept of being better by doing better.

48. You can start your life career while on drugs and alcohol but it's not possible to continue you life on career on rugs and alcohol and be successful because while the outside world doesn't know the issues, personal relationships suffer.

49. By being realistic, knowing and accepting the first step is "not easy, but very simple." After all, I took the first step by going on my own t receive detox and long-term treatment with the only desire at the end is to be a better person than when I started. I'm not going to make myself promises by saying I will never use drugs or alcohol again, but I will say I will use the tools taught to me and the resources provided to me to help me stay sober each day.

50. The time when I was brave was when I forgave myself.
Called my mother from detox and said, "Mom, I have to get help."
"I'm addicted to cocaine, and I don't wanna die."
When my mother visited Berkeley Medical Center, I looked her in the eyes.
Said, "I'm sorry for the pain I caused and I have to leave to get my life right."
This was the first time in many moons that honest words came from my mouth.

I apologized for lying to my family, and stealing from the house.

I didn't say I promise to not do drugs again or never have a drink.

I said, "I will give my best effort, and I love you. And please don't stop praying for me."

This is my story of bravery at two months clean.

Every night I pray for a day of sobriety so I can be the best version of me.

51. It doesn't bother if even one person puts shade on my gratitude while in recovery and relearning myself. I like to talk, think, and ask questions, and have discussions, so why would I not use my natural gift also also share my gift with others. I've heard it all, from "he's trying to run the group" or "he thinks he's better than others." Damn, did you ever think that maybe I believe in my recovery that much and if I do not participate and ask questions or express my opinions, ideas or feelings then I am placing a harm on my recovery by not communication with the person over the group and the other group members. I'm not afraid to be told I was wrong and given the right answers or being told other ideas. How can I help anyone if I won't be humble and take the time to absorb as much information as possible. There are some people who won't share anything without a catch attached to it. I wasn't raised to be that way and it takes one spark in one person's life to start real change or growth.

52. I'm one of those people who love the game and I studied the game but at the end of the day, I'm also a dope fiend dime-a-dozen. Just like the lady that took Daniel Boone to hear the truth, it took my aunt to tell me the truth and how it is, what it is and how I'm not fooling her or anyone else. Only people, I'm not fooling are the people doing the same fiend shit that I'm doing and I need to go to a 28-day-program and on day 28 ask myself if Ii'm ready to com home, got prison or stay another 28 days or however long it takes to get right, because all I'm doing is killing my mom and dad. Then she told me, "now if you wanna kill yourself, that's one thing, but don't bring everyone else down with you, and that's what's really going on."

53. I hear a lot about how the speakers at A.A. or N.A. are boring or having depressing realities until the person became clean using the 12 steps. I often question if I would get the same oppression and resistance when I share my story about addiction and recovery while searching for and growing my purpose. Yes, I can ask for support from a group I do not support. But is that right for me? Trust intertwines courage, morals, values, respect, honesty and integrity. Many times, as an addict, I would trust more into

the devils's playground, meaning drug dealers and addicts, than I did others. And if I have learned one thing about trust, I better start trusting that I am capable of changing, and even with trusting my recovery in other hands, there are boundaries and I must do the work. Please don't allow shame, embarrassment, or fear hold you back. More times than not, we will ask for a cigarette, food, a dollar, somewhere to sit, somewhere to shower, some to walk or ride with you, even someone to steal or scam with you or for you before asking a person who wants to help you stay sober for help with your sobriety and recovery. We have to stop being okay and content with what we know doesn't work. We are only making ourselves insane. And the definition if insanity is doing the same thing expecting different results.

54. Today is not going to be perfect. But each day that we breathe is a day that we are alive. There's no such thing as an immediate fix. We tried the immediate fix with drugs, alcohol, and other negative-addictive behavior. But everyday here in detox and substance-abuse long term care rehab is a day of faith in not only the program but in ourselves. No one can make you have faith in a higher power and no one can make you not have faith in a higher power either. Most of us put our higher power in a drink, on foil,

in our nose, in our mouth or in our veins, and we realized that that did not work out the best. So why not put our faith in a higher power that will help us to keep our temple, which is our body, healthy and clean. By doing this we help ourselves and possibly the next addict, or family member or person questioning having faith a higher power.

55. To be honest, my biggest trigger is me allowing myself to fall. I'm not falling anymore. I enjoy standing ten-toes-down and making sober-minded rational decisions and choices. God didn't take me this far to quit on life and God isn't thru with me yet. I'm going to make my daughter, Tany'Jah Hurshae' Ricks proud of her father with every moment of my life because she deserves better from me and I deserve better for myself.

56. On my left hand I have a Chinese symbol for Power with the word POWER under. I have had this tattoo since the year 2000. For me, POWER, is an acronym for People Often Wonder Even the Righteous. How many times have you gotten out of trouble and thanked God or got some extra money or things you wanted and thanked God? How many times have you thanked God for the things you need such as being able to breathe, taste, walk, listen

or learn. Many times, people question God when times are painful, unexplainable or when we feel things are not necessary or fair. Since the day I began recovery I have thanked God for my recovery and the recovery for everyone at The Oaks. Everyday and night, I asked God to give me strength to continue recovery. I believe my faith in my higher power is similar to my faith in recovery in the sense that I must work at it even when I don't want to. If I don't give my all then I can't expect to gain the help and guidance that I need. I love me and I know God loves me too. Faith is built day to day and not owed to me. I chose to use alcohol and drugs and live in the Devil's Playground so I have to work to stay out of the Devils's Playground and hustle smarter to avoid having alcohol and drugs and negative influences in my path to success, joy and peace.

> 57. Dear Addiction, without you, my life will be fine.
> I just had to take one step at a time.
> Even twice a day, a broke clock shows the right time.
> You're like mosquitos, and I invested in OFF.
> I no longer have to scratch after a bite.
> Or even get bit. My soul has the repellant.
> You no longer make me sick.
> Yesterday, I breathed better.

I have regained my scent and my sense.

I don't want a fifth, I'm good with my cup of
Joe, and a french vanilla blend.

Just know that God got us and we got God.

In the game of me versus addiction, there's no tie or
breaking even, I played my odds and won.

The first battle was rough in recovery and weighed tons.

That was day one.

There was blood, sweat, tears and fears the first month.

I went to a place out of my comfort zone, and you
would know that, coming from where I'm from.

For three months, I played solitaire like it was my addiction.

I picked up 52 cards and shuffled the deck, it was 1 in 1,024 odds.

My last week, I was stunned by how many matches I lit and won.

58. Our why, maybe one. Our why's maybe many. If we build the how, then our chances of survival open the opportunities of living. Just say no to drugs. Just say no to hate. Just say no to living a lie. Stop holding your gift to be accepted by people. Use your gift to motivate others. Use your gift to inspire you. Inspire yourself to the point that people who doubted you are now inspired by you. Yes, there will be pain. Yes, you will shed tears. Don't you deserve to be loved. Don't you deserve to be respected. The first thing to do is to make new habits. Make you respect you. If you have to

file down a pencil and use a corner of a piece of paper, write your name on that piece of paper, and before your name, write *I love you.* On the other side of the paper write *I love you,* and after that, write your name. Take that paper everywhere you go. Keep that reminder with you always.

59. To begin my discovery, I must first give a real effort to my discovery of life. I must challenge myself to a healthy, inspired recovery. We all know that A.A. is optional. I have to make a real effort to accept programs available for my recovery. I f I can't walk to recovery programs in the building I am in then it lowers the possibility of me traveling for recovery especially if I am not doing anything constructive at that time. If I only attend mandatory meetings then I am not being fully pro-active about my recovery. I've made time to use substances so why not put that same energy to my healthy recovery both physically and mentally.

60. *You gotta git up, git out and do something / don't let the days of your life past bye*

You gotta git up, git out and do something / don't spend all your time trying to get high.

Thees are the lyrics to Goodie Mob ft Outkast - "Git Up, Git Out." These lyrics are motivation to do a personal inventory of my life each morning to stay clean and be a productive person. I have to stay sober and mentally strong to make a difference in society and to push the culture forward.

61. If you are looking for a magic on / off switch, you are highly misinformed. Some days will be better than others. I feel it is hard to appreciate the good without the not so good times. Don't think that just because you stop using drugs and abusing substances that will be a peach. The goal is to work through our trials and tribulations with out searching for drugs and alcohol to resolve our issues and remove the pains of our realities of life. Find your higher power. Like 2Pac asked, "Who do you believe in. I put my faith in God, blessed and still breathin'.

62. This is my last Just For Today message to this group, but not my last Just For Today Message to myself. One thing about recovery is that we all started recovery alone. You must be able to push forward without me in the physical. You are strong enough to make it through recovery. For so long, you have been surviving

but now is the time for you to live and fall in love with living. So instead of me saying good luck, I'm a say, "I'll see you on the other side of addiction and that is living with recovery."

'

Made in the USA
Middletown, DE
04 April 2023

27744591R00031